The true story of the first Black Woman to graduate from a Nevada College.
Written by Dr. Jacqueline Parson Barker
Illustrated by Ricky Scott Holmes
Edited by Maryann Marsh

Published by a division of Parson's Legacy CDC
1757 Heather Oaks Way
North Las Vegas, Nevada 89031
702-321-7306
jparsonbarker@aol.com
Completed August 21, 2020
Final edit November 18, 2020

Foreword

This book is dedicated to my phenomenal mother, Stella Mae Mason Parson. She was the most amazing humanitarian, daughter, wife, mother, grandmother, counselor, spiritual advisor, teacher, and friend. Her life was God ordained and divinely directed. She was strategically placed and anointed to bring about permanent transformation. All who crossed her path were exceedingly blessed. We walked this life together. She was my mentor, my biggest fan, my best friend, my 24/7 and my everything. We literally did everything together! I was blessed by being able to serve her both spiritually and naturally.

First and foremost, I give all glory, honor and praise to God, his Son, Jesus Christ, and the power of the Holy Spirit. I am grateful for the ministering Angels that have been assigned to me. It is only through your favor and power that I'm able to achieve what YOU have purposed for my life.

I'd like to thank Patricia A. Green, Ed.D, for her encouragement and continuous friendship. Thank you to my husband, Eddie, for your constant support.

Last, but certainly not least, I'd like to thank my son, Antone Dotson-Parson.

He walked with me through this book every step of the way. He found the illustrators, the advisors, the publishers, and he most certainly did the marketing.

It is my prayer that everyone who reads this book will have a life-changing experience as you find and follow your Star.

Mama, because you were, I am. Because you did, I can. Because you would, I shall. Thank you Mama……

Chapter One

Stella sat in the dirt, in front of a little shack made of wood, staring at the stars. Today she saw her Mama crying as the plantation owner threw flour sacks at her feet and told her to use them to make clothes for her children; Mandy, L.J. (nicknamed Sonny Boy), W.M. (nicknamed Bugsy), Stella Mae, Nancy Lee and the baby, Vera Delores.

Her parents were sharecroppers in Mississippi. That meant they worked in the fields for the plantation owners in exchange for food, clothing and shelter. The whole family worked the farm from the youngest to the oldest, sick, and tired.

It was hard backbreaking work. At the end of the year the owner would add up all the hours the family had worked. He would then add what they owed him for food and shelter and subtract it from the total. What was left over was given to the workers in cash or trade.

Since the workers could not read, write, add or subtract, the owners often cheated them by telling them there was nothing left to give them. This was the case today. The owner told her father, Fred Mason, that they had not worked enough to get any money back. Stella's mama, Matilda, had high hopes that this year they had made enough money to move off the plantation and live on their own.

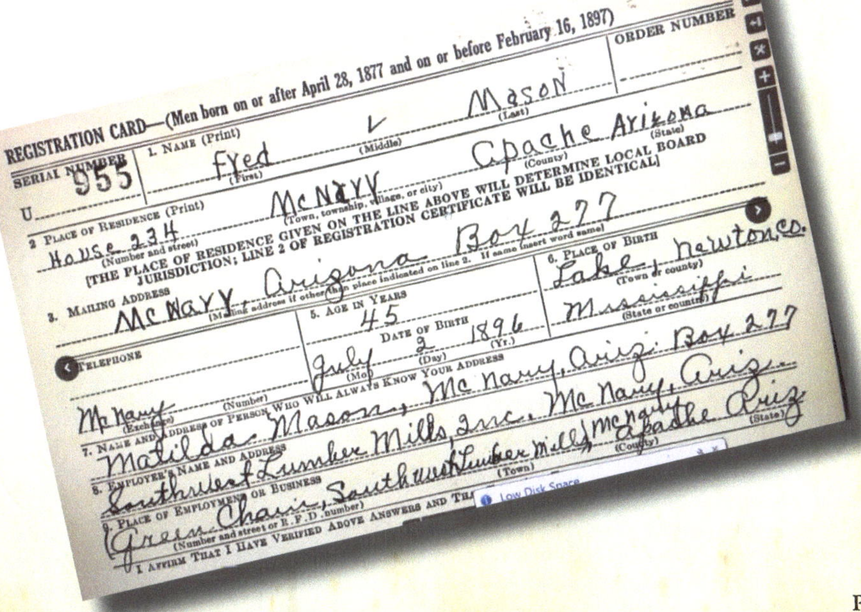

Devastated by the cruel injustices of the owner and the utter helplessness she felt, Matilda had humbly bent down and picked up the sacks. She would make them into coarse clothing for her six children.

Fred was more than hurt. He was angry and determined to get his family off this farm. The owner had told him that soon his daughters would be old enough to work in the main house. Fred knew that meant they could be treated in mean and harmful ways and he could not protect them.

This was to be the night. Stella overheard her daddy tell her mama that they would "steal away" from the plantation that night......in the pitch dark, under the stars. Stella's heart was anxious. Stella's heart was fearful. Stella's heart was excited.

Little did Stella know that one day she would become what her name meant in Spanish.......
a star!

So it was, in the dark of night, Stella's dad stole his family off the Kimbrew Plantation.

Chapter Two

That night, Stella's dad, made a daring move. He "stole" his family off the plantation and hid them with friends. It was a long, quiet, dark walk. They walked through towering trees lit only by the moon. Stella was sooo afraid. She remembered when Mr. Tom tried to run off. He got caught, and the plantation owners beat him badly. She could still hear his loud cries of anguish. But GOD was with the Mason family. Angels guided them safely to their place of refuge. There were friends waiting there to help them. The journey was not over. Stella's oldest brother, Sonny Boy, heard there was work out West for families of color. Sonny caught a ride heading West to see if he could find a new, safe life for his family, and he did. Sonny was brave. Sonny had hope. Sonny had God.

Chapter Three

McNary, Arizona was a mountain town that was mainly a lumberyard. Down South there was a McNary, Louisiana, which was a lumber town. When they had cut down all the trees, the owner, Mr. McNary moved to the thickly wooded mountain town in Arizona. He again named it after himself. Sonny Boy worked there until he saved up enough money to send a car back to get his father, Fred. Together they worked to save enough money to send a car for the rest of the family. They were happy. They were hopeful. They were free. Stella was on her way to see another kind of star.

Chapter Four

The road from Louisiana to Arizona was long, hot and hard. There were 17 people crammed into that car. There was no air conditioning. The kids had to sit on the floor between the sweaty stench of the adult legs. There were no motels or places along the way to shower or sleep. The drivers took turns driving straight through. Along the way they snacked on biscuits and salt pork wrapped in parchment cloth. Although it was a tortuously uncomfortable trip, the promise of a new life eased the pain. And so they arrived. They were together! There were ecstatic! They were family!

When they finally got to McNary, Arizona, they saw beautiful meadows and rolling mountains. There was a section behind one of these mountains where over 500 Black families lived. These families had been brought here by train from McNary, Louisiana to work the sawmills and railroads. They came with their goats and chickens and all their belongings to start a new life. Some say they were the first Black settlers in Arizona. Until they could build their own houses and grow their own vegetables, some lived in the boxcars of the trains. They were determined. They were adaptive. They were community.

Black men work inside the Basic Magnesium, Inc. plant in Henderson in this Dec. 3, 1942 photo. A large number of blacks migrated to Southern Nevada from the South during World War II because of jobs. *(photo from the Review Journey)*

News came that there were thousands of new, better paying jobs in a desert place called Las Vegas. There was a huge opportunity there. Workers were needed to build the Basic Magnesium Plant. Not only was the pay considerably higher but housing was provided for Black workers in a place called Carver Park. Upon hearing the news, the Mason family, along with many others, made their way to Las Vegas. This was finally home for the Mason family….

The home of Stella's Star! This felt right. This felt settled. This felt like home.

Chapter Seven

Las Vegas was a dry, dusty, hot desert. Blacks lived in tents, with dirt floors, on the west side of town. Sheets hung from the ceiling acting as room dividers. Food was cooked outside on a makeshift stove. The Outhouse, a little closet in the backyard, was where everyone went to potty. Some people might have seen this as being the poorest of the poor, but they were content and happy in their freedom. It was here that Stella really saw Stars! Eventually, Papa Fred, made enough money to buy materials to build a house. It was a small, two-bedroom house, with a kitchen, front room, back porch and an inside bathroom. Somehow, seventeen people lived in that one little house!

Stella was finally able to attend school. She and her sister Nancy walked five miles daily to get to the 5th Street K-8th grade school. Then they attended the 9-12th grade Las Vegas High School. Stella Mae had lots of friends because she was witty, friendly and fun. When Stella graduated, she became the first person in her family to get a High School Diploma. How proud her parents were! Stella was smart. Stella had dreams. Stella had purpose!

Las Vegas Highschool 1948

Like most Black girls of her time, Stella began to do what was then called "Day Work." That's when they would go into the homes of white ladies and do whatever was needed. Cook, clean, do laundry, babysit and whatever was required. She also worked as a waitress at a new Black-owned restaurant called Hamburger Heaven. Stella was a hard worker and a loyal family member. She was faithful to her church, working diligently in the choir and Sunday School. Her favorite hymn was "What a Friend We Have in Jesus". One of her favorite things to do at church was play the tambourine. Wow! She could really play that tambourine! A quick learner and an excellent orator, she stood out as a leader. Stella Mae, as some called her, knew that there was more for her. Deep in her heart she knew there was still a Star. She didn't know how, when or where, but she knew a door was opening that would lead her to that Star. Stella prayed that God would show her the way and worked while she waited.

One day it happened. A lady that she worked for, named Mrs. Ruymann, saw something in Stella Mae. She saw a woman who was quick-witted, humorous, and charming. She said, "Stella, you're too smart for this kind of work. I believe you can go to college and get a degree." Stella knew that her parents were too poor to send her to college. Her father had fallen ill and times were hard. Mrs. Ruymann was a member of an elite ladies group called the American Association of University Women. She told them about Stella and they agreed to give her a scholarship of $120 to attend college. There was only one college in the state of Nevada and it was 480 miles away. There was one more problem. No Black woman had ever attended this college. Most young Black women would have been afraid to attend an all-white college in 1948. It was not a very kind time for Blacks. It was not a very safe time for Blacks. It was not a very opportune time for Blacks.... but Stella saw Stars! She was brave. She was determined. She was chosen! So, she went on a train, all alone, very poor, with only a scholarship and a dream. It was daring. It was daunting. It was destined.

Chapter Nine

The University of Nevada Reno was a beautiful campus totally unlike the dry desert of Las Vegas. It was surrounded by lush greenery that was enriched by the bubbling Truckee River. This river flowed right through the middle of the campus, at one point overlooked by a small bridge. It was lovely and peaceful. Stella would have her challenges here. No white person could or would room with a black girl, so special arrangements had to be made. Stella stayed in a bare room alone with nothing but a bed and a chair. Reno had beautiful seasons with fabulously colored leaves, but the winters were very cold. Stella has no bedspread to put on her bed. She had no coat to put on to walk through the snow to class. She didn't even have 10 cents to buy a Coca Cola. Not one to pity herself, Stella got a job working on the Steam Tables serving meals to her fellow white students. This way she could eat free. On the weekends she would find work chopping firewood to heat the homes of people who lived in the city. Sometimes she would clean houses.... anything to get her through college. You see, the $120 was not enough to pay for everything, but it was enough to incite a dream within her. A dream to reach the stars. People back home would send Blue Chip Stamps to help her. These were stamps you earned when you bought groceries. After getting lots and lots of them you would put them into sticker books. After you fill up so many books, you could trade them in for money or shop for items. It was a challenging time. It was a lonely time. It was a determined time. Stella kept her head to the sky and her eyes on her guiding Star.

While in college there were some good things that happened. After two years, another Black woman enrolled in the college. She became Stella's roommate. Since her roommate's mother worked for rich white people, they gave Stella a coat and a bedspread. Stella was very grateful for these gifts! She had also made some white friends who were very nice to her. They wanted her to go out to eat with them. When the coffee shop wouldn't serve her, they all got up and left. Special arrangements had to be made for her to do her student teaching, because she was Black. She was accepted by a school and teacher that treated her well. Stella was a phenomenal teacher. Neither of them knew that she would one day receive many accolades for her award-winning teaching. She belonged to a loving church with people who knew her family and they embraced her and helped her all they could. God had prepared the way for Stella. She was in her last year of school, at the dawn of victory, when she got some devastating news.... her beloved father died. He would not be there to celebrate her historic march across the stage. Stella's Star had dimmed. Stella's Star had faded. Stella's Star was hidden behind a cloud of pain and despair. But God had a plan. It was at her father's funeral that Stella met a young Airman who had just been stationed at Nellis Air Force Base. Little did she know that he would cause her Star to shine again, more brightly than ever.

Chapter Ten

Stella returned to Reno with a heavy heart but determined to complete her education. And so it was, that in May of 1952, Stella became a Star. She marched across the stage to become the first Black Woman to graduate from any college in the State of Nevada. Her Star shone so brightly that it opened the doors for generations of young Black Women, including several in her own family. Every year, Stella gives a UNR scholarship to a struggling young Black woman. Fifty years later, on the Golden Anniversary of her degree, Stella was awarded the Presidential Medal of Honor. Her bravery, diligence, impact and influence had caught the attention of the world. She had succeeded against all odds. Stella Mae Mason Parson used her God given gifts, talents and wisdom to change the lives and direction of thousands of children and adults. This was her purpose and her destiny. Over the years she received numerous awards for her award-winning teaching and community service. After retiring from 33 years of of phenomenal teaching. Stella returned to college. She earned a degree in Marriage and Family Therapy and opened up a Counseling Center. In 1953, she married that Airman, Claude H. Parson, Jr., now an educator, and they had three children; Jacqueline, Naida Marie, and Claude III. Together they founded a church that birthed out over 60 ministries worldwide. The school district honored their commitment to serving and mentoring others by naming a public school in their honor. There is also a school in South Africa named after Mother Stella. The Church of God in Christ (over 8.5 million members in 102 countries) of which she was a lifelong member, named her one of the 150 most influential women. How amazing was her journey! God's hand was with that little Black sharecropper girl, who changed the world by following the Star. By the way, did I mention that the name Stella is Spanish for Star?

Gary Thompson/Review-Journal
STELLA PARSON: Never second-class
Black teacher
outlasts racism

Founders of Vegas View Church of God in Christ and over 60 branched out multigenerational ministries worldwide.

The community recognized their service by naming a school in their honor:
Claude and Stella Parson Elementary School

Empangeni,
South Africa

CHURCH OF GOD IN CHRIST
DEDICATED JUNE 15 1961
FRED MASON - TRUSTEE
C. COLEMAN - DEACON
C. E. COX - BISHOP OF NEVADA
H. MASON - SENIOR USHER

the
MASON-PARSON FAMILY
Legacy

One of Upper Room COGIC and Nevada First Jurisdiction's original founding families!
Deacon Fred Mason, Head Deacon and Trustee

Mother Matilda Mason, Head Church Mother
Arrived in Las Vegas in 1941!

Their Children:
Deacon L. J. (Mother Lula) Mason, Vegas View COGIC
Brother W.M. Mason (Robbie)
Asst. Supv. Nancy Mason (Pastor Leonard) Pleasants, Holy Temple COGIC, Reno
Evangelist Vera Delores Mason, Rehoboth Holy Temple COGIC, Reno
Vegas View COGIC Founders of Over 60 Ministries:
Asst. Supv. Stella Mason Parson,
Adm. Asst./Supt. Claude H. Parson Jr., and Elder Claude H. Parson III.

All ascended, but their influence continues through the Mason- Parson Legacy line.

Subject Integration

Math

What is the distance from Lake, Mississippi, where Stella was born, to McNary, Louisiana?

What is the distance from McNary, Louisiana to McNary, Arizona?

What is the distance from McNary, Arizona to Las Vegas, Nevada?

What is the distance from Las Vegas, Nevada to Reno, Nevada?

Add them all up to see the total amount of miles Stella traveled following her Star.

Science

Look up several uses of the chemical magnesium. What purposes do we use it for today? Do we have magnesium in our bodies? How does it help us physically? Research "Stars."

Reading Comprehension

Why was life better for Stella's family after they moved to Las Vegas?

What benefits did they have out West that they didn't have down South?

History

Track the years and important events of the Civil Rights Movement. Who were some of the key people who helped bring about positive changes for all people?

Social Studies

Why couldn't Stella eat at the diner with her white friends?

What does the word "Segregation" mean?

Is it right to treat people differently because they look different than you?

Why or why not? Do you have friends who look, act, speak, or dress differently than you?

Watch the Disney Movie "The Color of Friendship."

Music- Look up Stella's favorite song "What a Friend We Have in Jesus."

Art- Draw a picture of your favorite part of the story.

Physical Education- Stella had to walk five miles to school every day. Why is walking distances healthy for us? How much walking do you do each day?

Stella Mae's Star
Glossary of Terms

Plantation- a large area of land where crops are grown and tended by workers who live on the grounds.

Devastated- severe or overwhelming shock or grief

Injustice- not fair

Anxious- worried or nervous

Towering- extremely tall

Stench- bad smell

Ecstatic- overwhelming happiness and joy

Tortuously- in a very painful manner, difficult

Crammed- completely filled to the point of overflowing

Sawmills- a factory where logs are cut into lumber by machines

Magnesium- a chemical element with various uses such as light bulbs, alloy or aerospace

Diligently- doing something carefully and well

Orator- a great public speaker

Daunting- seeming difficult to do

Phenomenal- extraordinary, remarkable

Accolade- a reward or special honor

Influence- a person or thing that affects someone or something in an important way

Numerous- many

Parchment- non-stick paper used in baking

Opportune- well timed or useful

www.ingramcontent.com/pod-product-compliance
Lightning Source LLC
Chambersburg PA
CBHW040938110726
48006CB00001B/184